Animals and Us

Written by Jenny Feely

Series Consultant: Linda Hoyt

WorldWise
Content-based Learning

Contents

Introduction

The relationship that people have with animals is complex.

For more than 10,000 years people have tamed wild animals and bred them to suit their own purposes. Some **species** of animals have been changed in the process.

This book investigates many of the relationships that people have with animals and discusses how animals have been changed.

Chapter 1

From wild to domestic

Wild animals live, grow and **breed** without people being involved in any way. Wild animals flee from or may attack people if they come across them in the wild. People can tame wild animals, but it is quite difficult to do.

Domestic animals are not wild animals that have been tamed. Domestic animals have been bred to be comfortable living closely with humans.

Before animals were domesticated, people hunted and killed wild animals for food. This way of living was difficult and could be dangerous. People could not be sure they would find food every day. People were **nomadic**, moving from one area to another when the food ran out. This meant that they did not build permanent shelters. Over time, many people learned how to domesticate wild animals, and this changed the way people lived forever.

Domestic animals: Where did they come from?

	Wolf/Jackal	African wildcat	Asiatic wild horse	Urial
Ancestor				
Domestic animal	Dog	Cat	Horse	Sheep

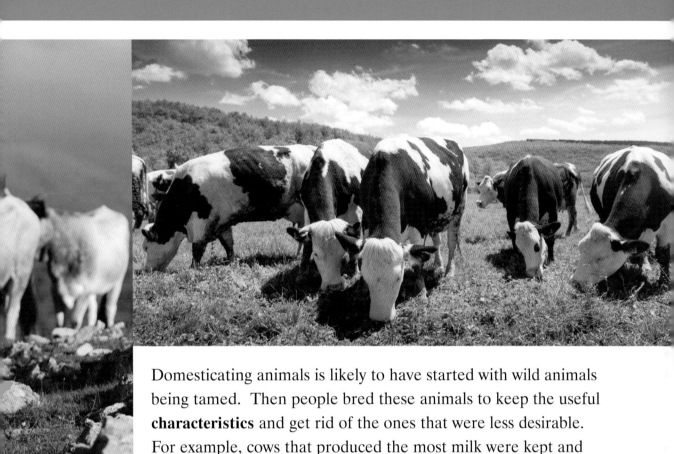

Domesticating animals is likely to have started with wild animals being tamed. Then people bred these animals to keep the useful **characteristics** and get rid of the ones that were less desirable. For example, cows that produced the most milk were kept and allowed to **reproduce**, in the hope that their young also produced a good supply of milk.

| Aurochs (extinct) | Wild boar | Persian wild goat | Red jungle fowl |
| Cattle | Pig | Goat | Chicken |

The first domestic animals

It is thought that dogs were the first animals to be tamed and then domesticated by people. Dogs were very useful to people since they could be trained to help with hunting. Over time, people learned to breed dogs so that they became more useful. Dogs that were good hunters were kept, but poor hunters were not. Dogs that could be easily trained were kept, but aggressive dogs were not.

Gradually, people learned to domesticate other animals. Goats, sheep, pigs and cows were bred to provide food such as milk and meat, and also leather for clothing. Animals such as donkeys, horses and camels could do heavy work such as ploughing, pulling wagons and carrying people. Later, other animals were domesticated for other reasons.

When were animals domesticated?								
Animal	Dog	Goat	Sheep	Pig	Cow	Cat	Donkey	Honeybee	Chicken
Date	15,000 BCE	10,000 BCE	8,000 BCE	8,000 BCE	8,000 BCE	7,500 BCE	4,000 BCE	4,000 BCE	3,500 BCE

6

Cats kept rats and mice out of food stores, silkworms produced fibres that could be woven into fabric, and many animals had warm fur that could be used for making clothing.

Changing ways of life

At the same time as people were learning to tame and then domesticate animals, they were also learning how to grow crops. These two developments changed the way that people lived very dramatically. Because they could now have a reliable source of food, people could stay in one place. They could build permanent houses to live in, and because they did not have to spend so much time looking for food, they had more time to develop other skills, such as making tools.

Think about ...

Zebras are a lot like horses and should be able to do the same work as horses. But zebras are much more skittish than horses – a trait that no one has been able to breed out of them.

Llama and alpaca	Silkworm	Camel	Horse	Turkey	Guinea pig	Rabbit	Mink	Hamster	Deer
3,500 BCE	3,000 BCE	2,500 BCE	2,000 BCE	CE100	CE 900	CE1500	1800s	1930s	1970s

7

What do domestic animals have in common?

Jared Diamond

There are many different types of animals in the world, but only a few of them have been domesticated. Historian and biologist Jared Diamond has proposed many new ideas about why some animals can be domesticated, and others cannot.

Diamond says that animals need to have the following characteristics to become domestic animals.

Characteristics of domestic animals

Easy to feed

Most domestic animals eat only plants or plants and meat. Meat-eating domestic animals such as cats and dogs can be fed scraps and parts of the animal that humans don't eat.

Pigs are fast-growing.

Grow quickly

It costs a lot to feed and look after an animal. Fast-growing animals reach a size where they can provide food or do work for people within a fairly short period of time.

Did you know?

Domesticating animals has led to an increase in the number of diseases that humans can get. For example, measles and tuberculosis have come to humans from cattle, influenza has come from pigs, and the common cold was first a disease of horses.

Breed easily in captivity

Many animals won't breed at all in **captivity**.

Easy to handle

An animal that is easily scared or very aggressive is difficult to work with and can be dangerous to people.

Not easily alarmed

Animals that are easily alarmed are difficult to farm. Gazelles have not been domesticated for this reason.

Belong to a herd or pack

An animal that lives in a herd or pack is used to being with other animals and recognises that the group has a leader. This allows a human to become the leader of the group and more easily able to move the group around. Bighorn sheep have not been domesticated because, unlike other sheep, they have no herd structure.

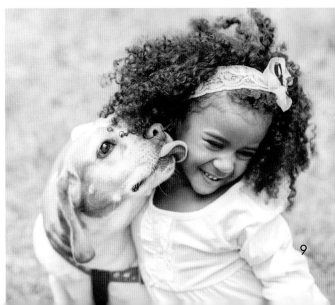

Domesticating the donkey

For thousands of years donkeys have been an important source of labour, transportation and even food for many people. The domestication of this animal has been very important to the development of civilisations around the world.

African wild ass

It is thought that the domestication of donkeys started in the area that is now the Sahara Desert. Ten thousand years ago this area was not a desert, but was covered in grasslands and had many lakes. People learned to domesticate cattle and kept them in herds that grazed on the Saharan grasslands. As the climate changed, the area became drier. This meant that the herders had to keep moving their cattle to find fresh grass and water.

Moving their families and the things they owned was difficult for the herders. It is thought that to solve this problem, these herders domesticated the African wild asses (donkeys) that grazed the grasslands with their cattle.

Donkeys were a good choice. They could carry children and small animals such as newborn calves and lambs easily so the whole family could travel with the herd. Donkeys could also carry water, firewood and grain.

Over the next 3,000 years, domesticated donkeys became prized possessions for many people. They were used to explore new lands. Donkey **caravans** enabled traders to transport large shipments of goods to other places and led to the development of trade routes and the exchange of ideas, goods and technology.

Today, while donkeys are still used for work in many countries such as India and the United States, more and more often they are being replaced by trucks and tractors. But many people still keep donkeys as pets.

Dogs at work

Domestic dogs are descended from wolves and are well suited to living with humans. They are pack animals, so they are used to having a leader to follow. They easily accept a human as the leader of their pack, which makes them good pets and work animals. People have trained dogs to perform many tasks.

▲ Farm dogs respond to whistles, spoken commands and hand signals, as they help the farmer move flocks of sheep or herds of cattle from place to place. This enables one farmer to manage large groups of animals.

▲ Police dogs also need to respond to commands so they can help police officers do their work. Police dogs help with many jobs, including catching people who are breaking the law and tracking criminals from crime scenes.

▼ Search-and-rescue dogs can follow scent trails to find people who are lost or who have been trapped, for example, in an earthquake.

▲ Sniffer dogs can smell illegal drugs even when the drugs are well hidden. Law enforcement agencies train dogs to sniff out chemical explosives that may be used in bombs. These dogs can detect about 19,000 different combinations of explosives.

▼ Therapy dogs visit people in health care centres such as hospitals and nursing homes. These dogs provide affection for the people in these places and sometimes help with physical therapy. There is evidence that these dogs can improve the health of patients and can reduce the need for medication for some patients.

▲ Guide dogs help blind and vision-impaired people to move around safely. Service dogs help people with physical disabilities. They are trained to open and close doors, pick up and carry things for their handlers, and even turn light switches on and off.

13

Chapter 2

Animals and diseases

Insects and disease

Insect bites can be itchy or painful, and sometimes they can be deadly. This is because some insects have microscopic **organisms** living in them that cause disease. These organisms don't harm the insect, but are very dangerous to humans. They can move from insects into humans when they are bitten by the insect. Diseases such as malaria, the Zika virus and yellow fever can all be caught in this way.

Scientists and doctors around the world are trying to stop the spread of these diseases. They hope to find:

- vaccines to prevent the spread of such diseases
- treatments to cure people who get these diseases
- methods for **eradicating** the insects that cause the spread of the diseases.

A lot of progress has been made in stopping the spread of insect-borne diseases, but many millions of people are still infected each year, and many die.

This map shows the level of risk of catching malaria in different parts of the world.

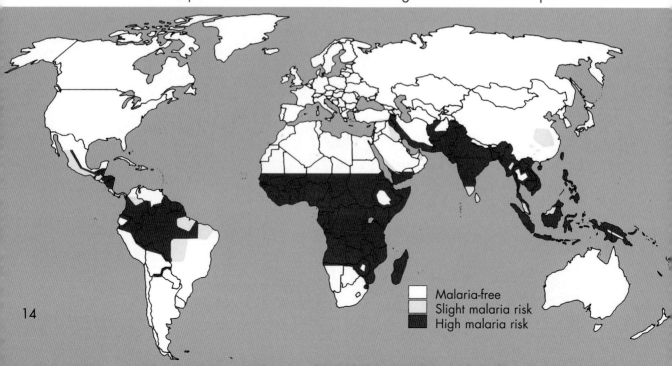

Malaria-free
Slight malaria risk
High malaria risk

Tsetse fly

The African tsetse fly spreads a disease called sleeping sickness. If untreated, this disease causes a slow and painful death. It is estimated that between 300,000 and 500,000 people contract this disease every year. Treatment is expensive and many people in Africa cannot afford it. International aid projects help to supply these drugs free of charge.

Tsetse fly

Assassin bug

In South America a small insect called the assassin bug spreads the deadly Chagas disease. Assassin bugs may bite humans and leave droppings containing a **parasite** on their skin. If the person scratches the bite, the droppings get mixed with the person's blood and the parasite enters and infects the body. The disease can be fatal if it is not treated.

Assassin bug

Fleas

A type of flea that lives on rats can spread a deadly disease called the plague. This disease has been responsible for millions of deaths throughout history and was often called the black death because it caused large black boils to erupt on the skin. One-third of the population of Europe died from the plague in the 14th century. While oriental rat fleas can still spread the plague, today it is treatable with antibiotics so it is not the terror that it once was.

▲ This picture from the 14th century shows a man suffering from the plague.

15

Mosquitoes

Mosquitoes can be annoying. They buzz around your ears at night and their bites can be itchy. However, in many countries, mosquitoes are more than annoying. One bite can cause a severe illness called malaria that can be fatal.

Malaria is caused by a tiny parasite called plasmodium, which is carried by some **species** of mosquitoes. This disease causes fever, headache, vomiting and other flu-like symptoms.

It is estimated that more than 1.5 million people die from malaria each year. There are treatments for malaria, but in places where malaria is common, such as Africa and Malaysia, many people cannot get or afford such treatments.

Mosquitoes can also spread other unpleasant diseases including yellow fever, dengue fever and the Zika virus.

Protecting against malaria

People can protect themselves against malaria by trying to avoid being bitten. They can do this by spraying **insecticide** around their houses and on themselves, having screens on windows and doors, sleeping under mosquito nets that have been treated with insecticides, taking medicine that prevents the disease and by killing as many mosquitoes as possible.

Governments and health organisations have established programs in many developing countries, where communities act together to try to eradicate mosquitoes. They try to stop the mosquitoes from breeding by destroying the habitats of young mosquitoes. They do this by spraying insecticides on **stagnant** water, filling in holes and ditches, covering water barrels and other water containers or putting oil on water.

 Did you know?

Although people can take medicine to prevent malaria, it needs to be taken every day. There is no vaccine available yet. If a vaccine were available, people would need only a small number of doses to be protected from malaria. This would be easier and cheaper than taking medicine every day.

Malaria facts

- Mosquitoes are most active around dusk.
- Only the female mosquito bites, because only the female feeds on blood. The female mosquito needs blood to develop its eggs.
- "Malaria" is an Italian word meaning "bad air". It was given this name because it was once wrongly thought to be caused by bad air around marshes.
- Malaria used to be found in the United States and Europe. Eradication programs have succeeded in getting rid of the disease from these places.
- Malaria is the most deadly of all tropical diseases caused by parasites.

Venom from animals: Killer or cure?

Most people stay away from poisonous animals because they fear getting a sting or a bite that could be very painful or even fatal. But some scientists get very close to poisonous animals so that they can study their venom. These scientists think that some parts of the venom could be used to treat human diseases such as cancer and diabetes or to help people who suffer from **chronic** pain.

Some types of venom work by **paralysing** the nervous system of the animal that is bitten or stung. By separating the part of the venom that causes the paralysis, scientists have found substances that can stop strong, ongoing pain in people.

A scientist milking a snake's venom

These are some of the ways that scientists are testing animal venom.

- Substances found in cobra venom are being tested for use as blood-thinning drugs to help prevent strokes in humans.

- A protein found in the copperhead snake's venom is being tested as a drug to stop **tumours** from growing.

- Venom from the South American rattlesnake is being investigated to see if it can be used as a strong painkiller.

- Bee venom has been used in alternative medicine for many hundreds of years. Scientists are currently researching its usefulness in the treatment of rheumatoid arthritis. It is thought that it may stop **inflammation**.

- Scorpion venom is being tested as a treatment for bone diseases such as arthritis. If successful, it could be used to stop this disease from weakening bones.

Cobra

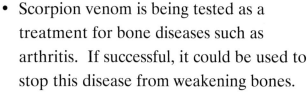

Scorpion

Chapter 3

Animals and science

Animal research

Animals are used in scientific research in many parts of the world. Sometimes the research is to find out more about the animals, but most often it is intended to find out more about how products, diseases and medicines might affect people.

The use of animals in medical research has led to many developments such as:

- medicines to treat infections and prevent diseases

- safer drugs for doctors to use to stop pain when operating on sick people

- insulin to treat diabetes

- organ transplants

- treatments for asthma, cancer and high blood pressure.

Some animal research focuses on ways to control or get rid of animals that are considered to be pests. A farmer might want to use a **pesticide** to stop insects from destroying a food plant, but would not want the pesticide to harm other animals on the farm. So researchers test pesticides on the target animal (for example, the insect) as well as on any other animal likely to be in the area where the pesticide will be used, such as birds and cattle.

In many countries there are laws that require animal testing of some products such as drugs. Such laws are intended to make sure that the drug works and to ensure that it won't harm people. Such products can be sold only if it can be proved that they will not hurt people. Since such tests cannot be carried out on people, the products and the materials they are made from are tested on animals. The results of these tests are used as proof of the product's safety. Without these laws, people would be at risk from harmful products.

▼ This farmer is spraying pesticide on a crop.

Did you know?

When penicillin was being developed as a treatment for infection, it was tested on mice. Before penicillin was discovered, a person could die from an infected cut. Since the discovery of penicillin, many more antibiotics have been developed and tested on animals.

21

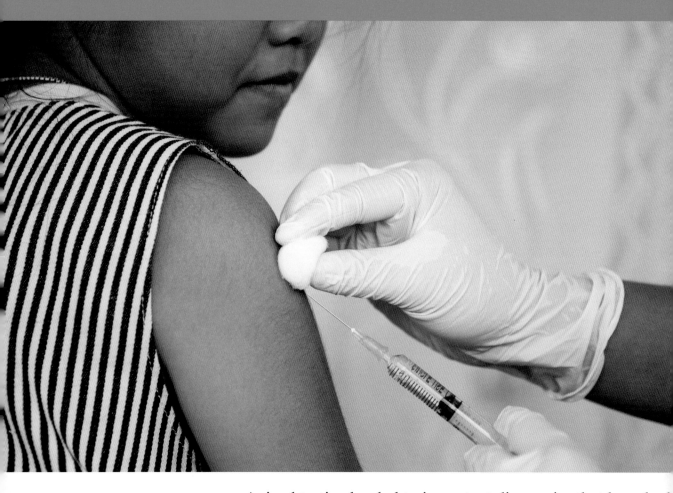

Animal testing has led to important discoveries that have had significant benefits for humans. But there is a lot of debate about the way animals are used in some research. Many people think that using animals in this way is, at best, stressful for the animals and, at worst, cruel.

Animal research numbers

No one knows for sure how many animals are used in research each year. This is because in many countries companies are not required to report how many animals they use for experiments. The RDS (Research Defence Society, an organisation in the United Kingdom that represents medical researchers) says it is likely that nearly 50 million animals are used each year in medical research.

 **Think about ...**

The average person eats more than 1,000 chickens in their life, but only two mice and one rat will be used in medical research per person.

22

The number of experiments being carried out on animals has decreased by 50 per cent in the past 30 years. Part of the reason for this is that more effective ways of testing have become available. For example, an Australian researcher has found that using human cells to find out how certain drugs affect the heart is more reliable than using animals.

Another reason is that the public opinion against animal testing has forced scientists to avoid using animals wherever possible. It is estimated that animal research makes up about 10 per cent of all medical research.

What products are tested on animals?

Animal testing has been used in the development of household products, cosmetics, agricultural chemicals, industrial chemicals, pesticides, paint and food additives.

Some products advertise that they have not been tested on animals.

▼ These people are protesting about using animals in experiments.

Chapter 4

Animals and the law

In many countries there are laws that protect animals from cruel treatment and ensure that they are looked after humanely. Under such laws, treating animals cruelly is not tolerated. But it was not always this way.

The history of animal rights

In 1822, a law outlawing cruelty to animals was passed in the United Kingdom. It was the first law of its kind and made it unlawful for anyone to beat, abuse or ill-treat working animals such as horses, sheep or cattle.

▼ This horse was ill-treated as it was not fed enough.

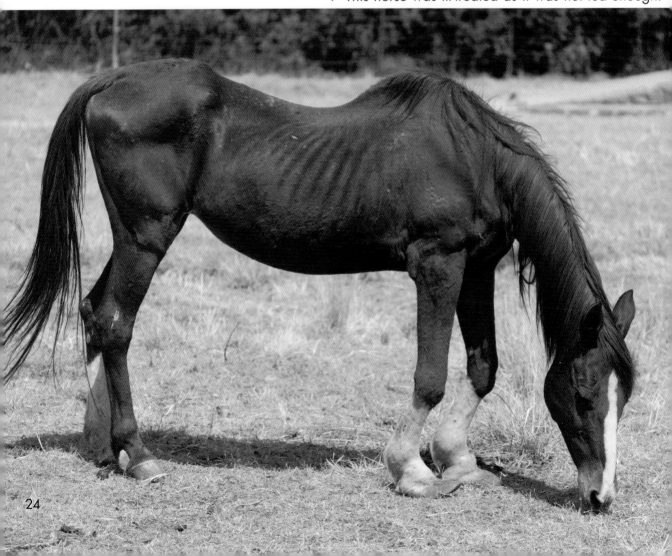

In 1824, the Society for the Prevention of Cruelty to Animals (later to become the Royal Society for the Prevention of Cruelty to Animals or RSPCA) was formed to support the enforcement of this law. Members of the Society inspected the markets and slaughterhouses and observed the way coach horses were treated.

Find out more

Are all animals protected by laws?

The establishment of the RSPCA in the United Kingdom inspired people in Australia who were concerned about animal welfare. Before long, animal welfare organisations were set up in each Australian city to protect animals from being misused. By the mid 20th century, each Australian state had a strong animal rights organisation, but it was not until the 1980s that the RSPCA became a national organisation. The RSPCA in Australia has continued the fight against animal cruelty and has been able to improve the way animals are treated in our society.

Around the world, many organisations have been formed to work for the rights of animals. One of these is PETA (People for the Ethical Treatment of Animals), which was formed in 1980 and has grown to be a huge worldwide organisation. PETA believes animals should not be used for food, clothing, entertainment or testing.

A protest against the wearing of fur

Animal rights in action

In San Francisco, a city in the United States, the practice of selling and slaughtering live animals changed after animal rights activists took Chinatown's market owners to court in 1998. Before this court case, market owners kept live animals in small tanks and cages and killed them when customers bought them. This was done so that buyers would know that the meat that came from the animals was fresh.

The activists argued that many animals were kept in cruel conditions where they did not have enough room to move – sometimes they were so crowded that animals were crushed. They claimed that the animals often did not have enough food and water. The court also heard that the animals were killed

inhumanely, with frogs being skinned and turtles being de-shelled while still alive. The activists were trying to get the sale of live animals banned on the grounds that this practice went against health codes and anti-cruelty laws.

The activists' case was dismissed by the judge, who ruled that people have the right to kill animals for food. He said he doubted that animals could feel pain, and therefore there was no basis for criminal charges to be made against the market owners.

However, after the court case, the activists and the market owners reached a compromise. They changed their practices so that animals were housed in larger, less crowded cages and were killed humanely.

Should animals have rights?

For thousands of years people have been talking about the place of animals in our world. Most people believe that animals should be treated humanely, but not everyone agrees about how humans should use animals. These arguments often focus on what rights animals have.

Arguments that presume animals have fewer rights than people raise the following points.

- Humans have always been hunters, and just as it is right for a tiger to hunt, kill and eat animals, it is also right for people to kill and eat animals.
- Humans have rights because they can distinguish between right and wrong. Animals cannot do this so they have no rights.
- Humans have power over all animals. It is reasonable to kill animals for food or to use them to develop products such as drugs and cosmetics that will improve or save the lives of people.
- People such as farmers, food producers and clothing manufacturers make their living from selling animal products. If animals were not used in this way, many people would be unemployed.

Arguments that presume animals have the same rights as people raise the following points.

- Humans have no right to use or abuse animals. Animals have the right to live their lives without interference from people, and it is wrong to eat, wear or use any product that has come from an animal or as a result of testing on animals.
- Just because animals cannot tell right from wrong does not mean they should not have rights. Babies have rights even though they are not old enough to know the difference between right and wrong.
- All animals can feel pain and should have the right not to be subjected to painful situations.
- Animals have moral rights because they are living things.

Not everyone sees the question as being so black and white. Some people believe that different animals have different rights. They think that those animals with the ability to learn, such as apes, chimpanzees, rats and mice, should have different rights than those that do not have this ability, such as insects and reptiles.

The issues surrounding animal rights raise many strong emotions and different points of view. It is a debate with convincing arguments on all sides. As well, it raises many complex issues. Perhaps it is a debate that will go on for thousands more years.

Conclusion

People first domesticated animals to provide food, and carry or pull heavy loads. Today, animals are still used for these reasons and more. Animals help us by doing dangerous jobs, by providing information for medical research and by assisting some people with disabilities.

The relationship between animals and people continues and will do so in the future. Most people appreciate the ways in which animals help us, but some people have mistreated animals. There are now laws to ensure that the rights of animals are respected.

 Think about ...

A mosquito lands on your arm and is about to bite you. What would you do?

Glossary

breed produce young

captivity being kept in an enclosed space

caravans groups of people travelling together

characteristics typical appearance or behaviour

chronic long-lasting and ongoing

eradicating getting rid of

inflammation redness and swelling of body tissue

insecticide a chemical used to kill insects

nomadic moving around from place to place without a permanent home

organisms living things

paralysing causing something to be unable to move

parasites animals, plants or funguses that live and feed on other living things

pesticide any chemical that is used by people to kill pests, such as insects on plants

reproduce produce young

species a group of animals of the same type that can reproduce with each other

stagnant standing still

tumours extra tissue that grows in the body

Index